FORM 19

OUR LIVING WORLD

Green Plants

By **Jenny Tesar**

With Illustrations by Wendy Smith-Griswold

Series Editor: Vincent Marteka
Introduction by John Behler, *New York Zoological Society*

A BLACKBIRCH PRESS BOOK
WOODBRIDGE, CONNECTICUT

Published by Blackbirch Press, Inc.
One Bradley Road, Suite 205
Woodbridge, CT 06525

Printed in Canada

10 9 8 7 6 5 4 3 2 1

Editorial Director: Bruce Glassman
Editor: Geraldine C. Fox
Editorial Assistant: Michelle Spinelli
Design Director: Sonja Kalter
Production: Sandra Burr, Rudy Raccio

Library of Congress Cataloging-in-Publication Data

Tesar, Jenny E.
    Green plants / by Jenny Tesar—1st ed.
        p.   cm. — (Our living world)
    Includes bibliographical references and index.
    Summary: Covers the metabolism, reproduction, and growth of green plants.
    ISBN 1-56711-039-8
    1. Plants—Juvenile literature. [1. Plants.] I. Title. II. Series.
QK49.T47   1993
581—dc20   93-8673
                                                                       CIP
                                                                        AC

Contents

What Does It Mean to Be "Alive"?

Introduction by John Behler,
New York Zoological Society

One summer morning, as I was walking through a beautiful field, I was inspired to think about what it really means to be "alive." Part of the answer, I came to realize, was right in front of my eyes.

The meadow was ablaze with color, packed with wildflowers at the height of their blooming season. A multitude of insects, warmed by the sun's early-morning rays, began to stir. Painted turtles sunned themselves on an old mossy log in a nearby pond. A pair of wood ducks whistled a call as they flew overhead, resting near a shagbark hickory on the other side of the pond.

As I wandered through this unspoiled habitat, I paused at a patch of milkweed to look for monarch-butterfly caterpillars, which depend on the milkweed's leaves for food. Indeed, the caterpillars were there, munching away. Soon these larvae would spin their cocoons, emerge as beautiful orange-and-black butterflies, and begin a fantastic 1,500-mile (2,400-kilometer) migration to wintering grounds in Mexico. It took biologists nearly one hundred years to unravel the life history of these butterflies. Watching them in the milkweed patch made me wonder how much more there is to know about these insects and all the other living organisms in just that one meadow.

The patterns of the natural world have often been likened to a spider's web, and for good reason. All life on Earth is interconnected in an elegant yet surprisingly simple design, and each living thing is an essential part of that design. To understand biology and the functions of living things, biologists have spent a lot of time looking at the differences among organisms. But in order to understand the very nature of living things, we must first understand what they have in common.

The butterfly larvae and the milkweed—and all animals and plants, for that matter—are made up of the same basic elements. These elements are obtained, used, and eliminated by every living thing in a series of chemical activities called metabolism.

Every molecule of every living tissue must contain carbon. During photosynthesis, green plants take in carbon dioxide from the atmosphere. Within their chlorophyll-filled leaves, in the presence of sunlight, the carbon dioxide is combined with water to form sugar—nature's most basic food. Animals need carbon, too. To grow and function, animals must eat plants or other animals that have fed on plants in order to obtain carbon. When plants and animals die, bacteria and fungi help to break down their tissues. This allows the carbon in plants and animals to be recycled. Indeed, the carbon in your body—and everyone else's body—may once have been inside a dinosaur, a giant redwood, or a monarch butterfly!

All life also needs nitrogen. Nitrogen is an essential component of protoplasm, the complex of chemicals that makes up living cells. Animals acquire nitrogen in the same manner as they acquire carbon dioxide: by eating plants or other animals that have eaten plants. Plants, however, must rely on nitrogen-fixing bacteria in the soil to absorb nitrogen from the atmosphere and convert it into proteins. These proteins are then absorbed from the soil by plant roots.

Living things start life as a single cell. The process by which cells grow and reproduce to become a specific organism—whether the organism is an oak tree or a whale—is controlled by two basic substances called deoxyribonucleic acid (DNA) and ribonucleic acid (RNA). These two chemicals are the building blocks of genes that determine how an organism looks, grows, and functions. Each organism has a unique pattern of DNA and RNA in its genes. This pattern determines all the characteristics of a living thing. Each species passes its unique pattern from generation to generation. Over many billions of years, a process involving genetic mutation and natural selection has allowed species to adapt to a constantly changing environment by evolving—changing genetic patterns. The living creatures we know today are the results of these adaptations.

Reproduction and growth are important to every species, since these are the processes by which new members of a species are created. If a species cannot reproduce and adapt, or if it cannot reproduce fast enough to replace those members that die, it will become extinct (no longer exist).

In recent years, biologists have learned a great deal about how living things function. But there is still much to learn about nature. With high-technology equipment and new information, exciting discoveries are being made every day. New insights and theories quickly make many biology textbooks obsolete. One thing, however, will forever remain certain: As living things, we share an amazing number of characteristics with other forms of life. As animals, our survival depends upon the food and functions provided by other animals and plants. As humans—who can understand the similarities and interdependence among living things—we cannot help but feel connected to the natural world, and we cannot forget our responsibility to protect it. It is only through looking at, and understanding, the rest of the natural world that we can truly appreciate what it means to be "alive."

1

Green Plants: The Overview

Try to imagine a world without green plants. No grass or trees. No rosebushes or potato plants. No ferns or tulips or ivy. And no animals such as ants, woodpeckers, sheep, lions, and gorillas!

You may not realize it, but you—and every other animal—owe your life to plants. Without green plants, nothing could exist. Humans and other animals cannot live without food and oxygen, and they cannot make these things on their own. They depend on green plants to produce both of these essentials. In the presence of light, green plants are able to produce their own food by turning water and carbon dioxide into sugar, which is the simplest food. In the process, they release oxygen into the air.

People and other animals breathe air for oxygen. They eat plants for food—or they eat animals that eat plants. If all the green plants disappeared, people and other animals would soon starve to death.

Opposite:
Brilliantly colored California poppies cover a field in Antelope Valley, California. Without green plants, animal life on Earth would not be possible.

What Is a Plant?

It is easy to see that a dog is an animal and that a dogwood tree is a plant. But what makes a coral an animal and a moss a plant?

All living things are made up of tiny building blocks called cells. Plant cells do not look like animal cells. They have thick walls that are composed of a material called cellulose. Animal cells do not have cellulose or walls.

Some plant cells, especially those in leaves, contain a green substance called chlorophyll. Only cells with chlorophyll can make food—in a process called photosynthesis. Animal cells have no chlorophyll.

Plants do not move from one place to another. They spend their entire life in one spot. In contrast, most animals can move about. They have muscles and nerves that make this possible. Plants do not have muscles or nerves.

Another difference between plants and animals is their manner of growth. An animal grows until it reaches a certain size and form that is typical for its species. After that, the animal changes very little during the rest of its life. For example, most humans grow until they are 5 to 6 feet (2 meters) tall. They reach this height when they are in their teens and do not grow taller, even though they may live another 70 years. A plant often has unlimited growth, continuing to grow throughout its lifetime. There are trees that are still growing taller and wider even though they are thousands of years old!

The Amazing Variety of Green Plants

Scientists have identified about 400,000 kinds, or species, of green plants. The greatest number of these—about 250,000 species—are flowering plants. The rest are mainly conifers, ferns, and mosses.

Some flowering plants are trees—such as the brilliant pink magnolia. Of the approximately 400,000 kinds of green plants, the majority are flowering plants.

Flowering plants Flowering plants reproduce by means of seeds. The seeds are enclosed in a fruit that develops from part of the flower. Only flowering plants have fruits and flowers.

Flowering plants come in an endless variety of shapes and sizes, but they all have roots, stems, leaves, and flowers. The leaves are usually broad and flat. Inside the plant's body is a system of tubes called the vascular system. These tubes carry water and food throughout the plant's body, much in the way that the circulatory system carries water and food throughout the human body.

Some flowering plants, such as magnolias and oaks, are trees. They have a single woody stem called the trunk. Other flowering plants, such as roses and lilacs, are shrubs. They are smaller than most trees and have many woody stems. Shrubs are also known as bushes.

Green Plants: The Overview

Conifers, such as these blue spruces, are cone-bearing plants. Most conifers prefer cool climates and are called evergreens because they keep their leaves all year long.

Ferns have delicate, feather-like leaves and prefer moist, shady environments.

Herbs do not have woody stems. Their stems are rather soft and are not thick. Herbs are smaller than trees and shrubs. Grasses, beans, mints, marigolds, and carnations are examples of herbs.

Flowering plants can be found almost everywhere on Earth. Some kinds live in warm, moist jungles; others live on cold mountains or in dry deserts. There are green plants in swamps, in ponds, in cities, on Arctic plains, and along the edge of oceans.

Conifers Pines, spruces, and cedars are examples of conifers, or cone-bearing plants. They reproduce by means of seeds that form in wood-like cones. Like flowering plants, conifers have a vascular system, with roots, stems, and leaves. The leaves are narrow and hard and are shaped like needles or scales.

Most conifers are trees, but some are shrubs. They grow mainly in cool places, such as Canada and northern Europe.

Ferns It is easy to recognize a fern. Most ferns have broad feather-like leaves. Ferns are vascular

plants with roots, stems, and leaves, but they do not produce seeds. They reproduce by means of spores. On the underside of a fern leaf there are small brown dots. These dots contain the spores. The majority of ferns grow in moist, shady places and are most abundant in tropical forests.

Mosses are among the smallest green plants. They live in moist places, such as damp forests, where they grow on top of many surfaces, including rocks, soil, and trees.

Mosses Some of the smallest green plants are mosses. They have no vascular system. Without any special network to carry food and water, mosses can't grow very tall. Food and water have to seep from one cell to the next, and this is a slow process.

Mosses do not have true roots, stems, or leaves, but they have parts that resemble those features. Mosses grow close together, forming mats, or clumps, along the edges of streams and in other moist, shady places. Like ferns, mosses reproduce by spores.

Green Plants: The Overview

The Short and the Tall of It: Record-Holding Plants

Giant sequoias are the largest green plants and the heaviest living things ever to have existed on Earth.

Some green plants are very tiny. A duckweed is not much bigger than the head of a pin. At the other extreme are the giant sequoias of California. The largest sequoia even has a name: The General Sherman tree. It is named after William T. Sherman, a famous Civil War army officer. The base of the General Sherman's trunk is 36 feet (11 meters) across. The tree is more than 272 feet (83 meters) high. Scientists estimate that it weighs more than 6,000 tons (5,000 metric tons). Sequoias are the heaviest living things ever to have existed on Earth. They are also among the oldest. The General Sherman tree is thought to be about 3,500 years old!

The prize for tallness goes to a relative of the sequoia: the coastal redwood of California. One coastal redwood was reported to measure 385 feet (117 meters) tall. Another very tall tree is a species of eucalyptus that is native to Australia. It grows to more than 370 feet (113 meters) high.

The tree with the biggest spread is the banyan. The banyan is a type of fig tree native to India. As a banyan gets bigger, roots grow down from its branches. When these "pillar roots" reach the

ground, they grow into the soil and look just like tree trunks. As the branches grow longer, they continue to produce more pillar roots. One particular banyan in India has more than 1,000 pillar roots and has spread so far that 20,000 people could stand beneath it!

The world's largest leaves belong to raffia palms of Africa. One of these feather-like leaves can be more than 65 feet (20 meters) long. Another plant with huge leaves is South America's Victoria water lily. Its leaves may be more than 6 feet (2 meters) across—and strong enough to float a small child.

The largest flowers are made by rafflesia. This Southeast Asian plant lives mostly underground, stealing food from the roots of other plants. But its giant red flower forms above ground. The flower may be 4 feet (1 meter) across and may weigh up to 25 pounds (11 kilograms). In contrast, duckweed flowers may be only 1/50 inch (1/20 centimeter) across. You would

The world of green plants is filled with organisms of incredible variety. *Top left:* Bristlecone pines of California can live as long as 4,600 years and are among the oldest living things on Earth. *Top right:* The leaves of the Victoria water lily may grow up to 6 feet (2 meters) wide. *Bottom left:* The largest flowers produced by any green plant belong to the rafflesia of Southeast Asia. Its flowers can grow up to 4 feet (1 meter) wide and can weigh up to 25 pounds (11 kilograms). *Bottom right:* The banyan tree of India has the widest spread of any plant because many of its roots grow down from its branches.

The Parts of a Flowering Plant

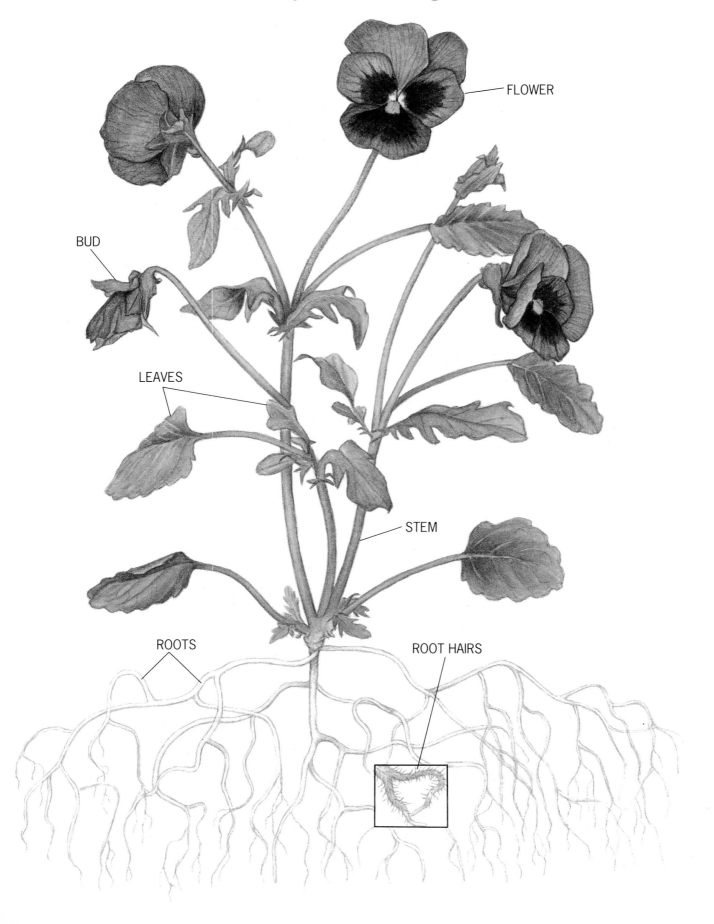

FLOWER

BUD

LEAVES

STEM

ROOTS

ROOT HAIRS

have to line up more than 2,000 duckweed flowers to equal the diameter of one rafflesia flower!

Even older than the General Sherman tree is the bristlecone pine—one of the oldest living things on Earth. It grows very slowly, but it can live as long as 4,600 years! Most trees live only 100 to 250 years.

The Parts of a Plant

The body of almost every vascular plant consists of three main parts: roots, stems, and leaves. Each of these parts has important functions that help the plant survive. Together, they take care of the plant's everyday needs.

Roots The roots of most plants are underground. As they grow, they may branch again and again until they have spread far from the stem. Some plants have fibrous roots. Their root systems have many thin branches, which are about equal in length and thickness and which spread out in many directions. Rye and other grasses have fibrous root systems. Other plants, such as dandelions and carrots, have taproot systems. These plants have one large main root, with many smaller roots branching from it. Unlike fibrous roots, taproots grow straight down.

The depth of a plant's roots doesn't necessarily relate to the size of the plant's above-ground parts. For example, scientists who studied one rye plant that was only about 20 inches (51 centimeters) tall found that it had 380 miles (611 kilometers) of roots! Roots have three jobs: to anchor the plant, to absorb water and minerals from the soil, and to store food.

The roots of a plant hold it in the ground. This prevents the plant from being blown away by high winds or washed away by floods.

Plant roots also absorb, or take in, water and minerals from the soil. A plant needs water and

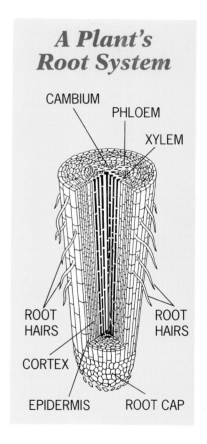

A Plant's Root System

CAMBIUM
PHLOEM
XYLEM
ROOT HAIRS
ROOT HAIRS
CORTEX
EPIDERMIS
ROOT CAP

High Tops

Orchids are among the most beautiful and colorful of all plants. Most orchids do not grow in the ground. Instead, they grow on tree branches high above the ground in warm, moist rain forests. Orchids anchor themselves to the tree branches with their roots, which absorb water from the air and take in minerals from dead leaves and other debris that become trapped between the roots and branches.

Orchid

DID YOU KNOW

Barking Up the Right Tree

Sequoias are incredible plants in many ways. One reason they can live for thousands of years is that their super-thick bark protects them against many dangerous elements, including fire. Some old sequoias have bark that is more than 2 feet (0.6 meter) thick!

Strawberry plants have stems called runners that grow horizontally along the surface of the ground.

minerals to make food, and therefore to survive, just the way animals do. The tip of a plant root is covered with a fuzz of tiny hairs. It is in these root hairs that all absorption of water and minerals takes place. The root hairs work with the vascular system, which in turn carries the water and minerals up to the stem and the leaves.

The roots of some plants, such as beets, carrots, and radishes, store food for the rest of the plant to use. At night, and at other times when the plant cannot make enough food to meet its needs, it survives by using some of the stored food.

Stems Most plants have stems that grow upward from the roots. Part or all of the stem may be underground. Other plants, such as ivy, have special

16

Green Plants: The Overview

stems called tendrils that trail along the ground. These plants climb fences and other solid objects by winding their tendrils around the objects. Strawberry plants have stems called runners that grow horizontally along the surface of the ground. Potato plants have underground stems—the round, swollen ends of these stems are the potatoes you eat.

The stems of some plants, like asparagus and tulips, are soft and green. Other plants, including all trees, have woody stems covered with a tough bark. The bark protects the tree against temperature extremes, fire, and insects that bore into the wood.

The stems of trees are woody and are covered with a thick, tough skin called bark.

Like plant roots, the stems of a plant also have important jobs to do. The stems carry food to all parts of the plant. Water and minerals move from the roots upward through the stem. Food materials move from leaves downward through the stem. The stems of some plants—those with soft green stems and desert plants—actually make the food because they contain chlorophyll. The stems also act as supports. They hold the leaves up to the light, which is necessary for the leaves to make food. They also hold up flowers and fruit.

Leaves make food for green plants. Filled with chlorophyll, a green substance, the leaves absorb sunlight to make glucose, nature's most basic nutrient.

Leaves Leaves come in many shapes and sizes, but they have one important function: to make food. Some leaves also have other functions. Sweet-pea

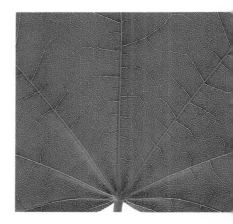

Green and Keen

Have you ever seen green scum on the surface of a pond? Have you seen seaweed in the ocean? The scum and seaweed are types of algae. Almost all algae live in water. Some algae consist of just one cell. They are so tiny that they can be seen only through a microscope. Seaweeds are the biggest algae. One seaweed, the giant kelp, may be 100 feet (31 meters) long.

Like plants, algae contain chlorophyll, the green substance needed to manufacture food. Animals that live in water depend on algae for food. Some animals eat algae. Other animals depend on algae indirectly, eating animals that eat algae. A big fish feeding on smaller fish that have eaten algae is an example of indirect feeding.

Algae are very simple organisms. They have no roots, stems, leaves, flowers, or cones. They are made up of either one cell or only a few kinds of cells. Many species do not look anything like plants. Some one-celled species have tails called flagella. They can swim about in the water, much like an animal.

Scientists, who used to divide living things into two kingdoms—animals and plants—classified algae as "simple plants." Since algae, and some other organisms, do not really fit into either kingdom, algae are now placed in a separate kingdom within a five-kingdom classification system and are considered neither plants nor animals.

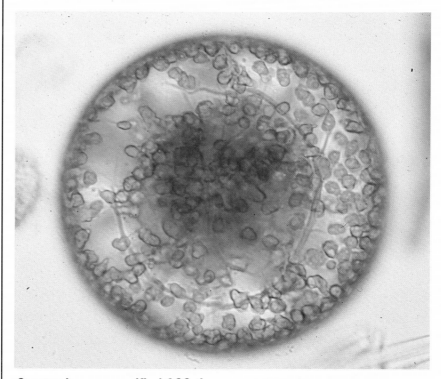

Green algae, magnified 100 times

leaves form tendrils that attach the plants to supports. Cactus leaves are spines, which protect the cactus stem. The spines do not make food; food making takes place in the stem of the cactus.

The History of Plants

Life on Earth probably began more than 3 billion years ago. The earliest living things were one-celled organisms that lived in the sea. The land was lifeless.

Gradually, over millions and millions of years, some living things changed, or evolved. New kinds of organisms developed. The first land plants appeared about 430 million years ago. They did not look like the plants we see today. They were very simple, with horizontal stems, upright branches, and no leaves or flowers. We know of their existence because they left behind fossils—the remains, or traces, of ancient organisms.

It is from these fossils that we also know that forests of giant tree ferns grew in North America about 300 million years ago—long before there were people and other mammals. The tree ferns lived in swampy areas. As they died, they sank to the bottom of the swamps. Through millions of years, more and more tree ferns and other green plants fell, squashing the plant matter underneath. As a result of changes in the Earth's climate, the swamps dried up, and the tree ferns died. The thick layers of dead tree ferns were eventually turned into beds of coal.

Then the first conifers appeared. They were most abundant about 225 million years ago. Next came the flowering plants, which have been on Earth for about 120 million years. In time, more and more plant species developed, many of which look much like our present-day specimens. Today, all parts of the Earth contain some kind of green plant.

2

Reacting to the Environment

Like animals, plants must constantly gather information about their environment. Plants detect changes in their surroundings that are important to survival. You can see how a plant plays detective by doing a simple experiment.

Place a begonia on a sunny windowsill, and keep it there for a while. After a few days, you will notice that all the leaves have turned toward the window. Then turn the begonia around so all the leaves are facing into the room. In a day or two, the leaves will have turned around to face the window. This tells us that light is important to a begonia. The begonia leaves changed direction because the plant needs light in order to make food.

A change in the environment that can be detected by a plant is called a stimulus. To stay alive, a plant must be able to react to stimuli. The reaction that a plant makes to a stimulus is called a response.

Opposite:
All living things must react to their environment in order to survive. One way that plants react to their surroundings is by bending their leaves toward a source of light.

Plants and animals detect and respond to stimuli differently. Most animals have sense organs, such as eyes and ears, that detect stimuli. From these organs messages are carried to the nervous system. The brain, which is the main organ in the nervous system, then sends a signal to the animal's muscles. An animal responds by moving muscles. Plants do not have sense organs, a nervous system, or muscles. In ways not yet completely understood, plants receive stimuli through certain cells, such as those at the tips of roots and stems. Chemical messages or electrical signals are sent to other cells, which respond to the stimuli. Some plant responses are called tropisms. Others are called turgor movements.

Tropisms

The main way that a plant reacts to a stimulus is by bending toward it or away from it. A movement such as this is called a tropism. The word comes from a Greek word that means "a turning."

Bending is controlled by chemicals known as auxins. When an auxin concentrates in certain cells, it causes the cells to grow longer. Consider what happens when a begonia plant is laid on its side. At first, all the stems are horizontal. Soon, however, auxins concentrate in the cells on the lower side of each stem. As a result, the cells on this side grow much faster than the cells on the upper side of the stem. Because the two sides of the stem grow at different rates, the stem begins to bend.

Tropisms can be positive or negative. When a plant's leaves bend *toward* a stimulus such as sunlight, that is a positive tropism. When the plant part bends *away* from the light, that is a negative tropism.

Reactions to light Bending in response to light is called phototropism. Stems and leaves will react

Brrrrr! It's a chilly winter morning. What do you do when you want to know how cold it is outside? Perhaps you listen to the weather report on the radio or read a thermometer. But, if there's a rhododendron in your garden, you could use it as a thermometer.

Rhododendrons are attractive shrubs with dark, shiny leaves. The leaves remain on the shrubs all year round, even when the ground is covered with snow. To learn how cold it is, you can look at the rhododendron's leaves.

During warm weather, when temperatures are 60 degrees F. (16 degrees C.) or higher, rhododendron leaves lie almost straight out. As temperatures fall, the leaves begin to droop and curl. The colder the temperature, the more they droop. At 20 degrees F. (-7 degrees C.), the leaves hang almost straight down and are tightly curled.

How do the leaves hang at 40 degrees F. (4 degrees C.)? At 0 degrees F. (-18 degrees C.)? If you have a rhododendron, watch it to find out! Soon you'll be looking at the plant instead of the thermometer to learn the temperature.

Rhododendron

positively to light. They grow toward light because they need light to make food. Roots, however, react negatively to light by growing away from it. If a root is pulled out of soil and placed on a surface where it is kept moist, its tip will grow into the soil.

The auxin that reacts to light actually moves away from light and concentrates in shady areas. When a begonia is turned around in a windowsill, auxin begins to move from one side of a stem to the other. It moves away from the sunny side to the shady side.

Reactions to gravity Another important plant stimulus is gravity. Gravity is a force, or pull, exerted by the Earth's mass. Bending in response to gravity is called gravitropism, or geotropism.

Stems show negative gravitropism. They grow upward, away from the source of gravity. Roots have positive gravitropism. They grow downward, toward the source of gravity. These reactions ensure that the

Leaf Me Alone

A hungry insect lands on a tree and begins to eat its juicy leaves. The tree quickly reacts by pouring bad-tasting chemicals into its leaves. The insect flies away to another tree, but it's too late. The first tree has warned its neighbors, and they have already begun pouring bad-tasting chemicals into their leaves.

Does this sound like science fiction? Perhaps, but it actually happens. Gordon Orians and David Rhoades, scientists at the University of Washington in Seattle, discovered that Sitka willows produce a poisonous chemical when they are attacked by leaf-eating caterpillars. The chemical is carried by the wind. When it reaches other Sitka willows, they respond by increasing the amount of chemical in their leaves.

Jack Schultz, a scientist at Dartmouth College in Hanover, New Hampshire, found that sugar maples, red oaks, and poplars also communicate chemically. Do all plants produce chemical messengers? Are these messengers produced only to warn other plants, or do the messengers have other uses? Scientists are working to answer such questions.

leaves will be exposed to light and air, and the roots will be in soil, where they can take in nutrients.

One of the best ways to see gravitropism at work is to watch a plant sprout from a seed. When the plant begins to grow out of the seed, it forms a tiny shoot and a tiny root. The shoot grows up, and the root grows down. This happens even if the seed is sideways or upside down.

Reactions to other stimuli Water is also an important stimulus. Roots respond positively to water. Cells in the growing areas of the roots bend so that the roots grow toward water.

Many climbing plants, such as sweet peas and morning glories, have tendrils that wrap around poles and other objects—much like a monkey's tail wraps around a tree branch. The tendrils help support stems as they grow upward.

Tendrils respond positively to touch. As they grow, they constantly make circular movements. When a moving tendril touches a pole, its growth changes. Cells on the side away from the pole grow very fast. This causes the tendril to curl around the pole. The unattached part of the tendril also forms a coil. This pulls the plant closer to the pole.

Good examples of chemical tropisms are seen in flowers. For seeds to form, pollen from a flower must

Morning glories, like most climbing plants, have tendrils that wrap around supporting structures to help the plant grow upward.

land on the top of the female part of another flower of the same species. Then a pollen tube must grow down the female part to the ovary. Will begonia pollen that lands on the female part of a rose, for example, grow downward? The answer is no. For begonia pollen to grow, it must receive a chemical message that says, "This is the female part of a *begonia* plant."

What makes the tube grow downward, rather than sideways? The tube grows toward calcium, which is more concentrated in the ovary than anywhere else in the female part of the flower.

Turgor Movements

Some plant reactions depend on changes in internal water pressure. These are called turgor movements. Chemical messengers or electrical signals cause cells to gain or lose water. As a cell takes in water, it becomes stiff. As it loses water, it becomes limp. Turgor movements are much faster than tropisms. Some take only a second or two. Turgor movements in the mimosa and Venus's-flytrap are among the most awesome. The leaves of both these plants instantly react to touch.

Leaf folding Sometimes called the sensitive plant, the mimosa has small feathery leaves. Each leaf consists of many tiny leaflets on a central rib. When something touches part of a leaf, all its leaflets quickly fold up. Whatever touches the leaf—the stimulus—causes an electrical message to be sent to

DID YOU KNOW

Nap Time

Unlike animals, plants do not have eyes that they can close, but some of them look as though they're sleeping. The oxalis plant, for example, which grows mainly in Africa and the warm parts of America, has leaves that close up at night and open in the morning.

Mimosa leaves are very sensitive to touch. As soon as they come into contact with a stimulus, electrical impulses in the plant tell each cell to shed water, which makes the leaves go limp.

Venus's-Flytrap: A Big Surprise for Flies

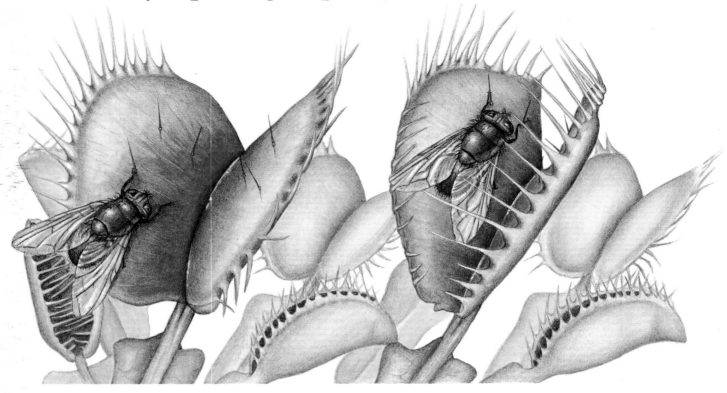

A fly lands on the plant, touching the sensitive hairs.

Chemical reactions in the hairs send electrical signals to the hinge, telling it to close.

cells at the base of each leaflet. These cells lose water and become limp, causing the leaflets to droop. In 10 to 20 minutes, if the leaf is not disturbed, the cells begin to take in water. As they become stiff, the leaflets return to an open position.

For some kinds of mimosas, leaf folding may be a method of defense. These mimosas have sharp thorns on their branches. When the leaves fold up, the plant's thorns are exposed. This makes it easier for the thorns to puncture the tongue or skin of a hungry animal, for example.

Leaf closing Venus's-flytrap is a small plant that lives in swampy places in the southeastern United States. In addition to making food, it traps and eats insects. This gives the plant nitrogen, which it needs to make protein. The soil where Venus's-flytraps live does not contain much nitrogen.

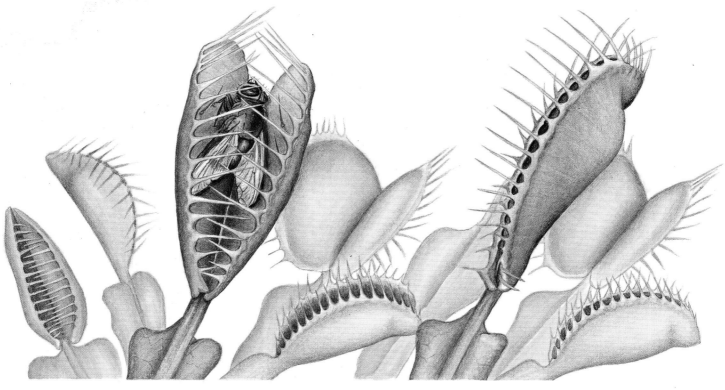

In an instant, the fly is trapped inside the plant.

Digestive juices pour out of the leaf and begin to break down the insect's body. The leaf will reopen in 7 to 10 days.

A Venus's-flytrap leaf has two halves that are hinged together. Each half has a row of sharp bristles and three very sensitive hairs. When an insect crawls along the top of the leaf, it touches one or more of the hairs. Chemical reactions take place in the hairs and send electrical signals to special cells in the hinge. The cells quickly stiffen as they swell up with water. This causes the two halves of the leaf to snap shut. In a split second, the insect is trapped inside the plant, between the two halves.

Digestive juices then pour out of the Venus's-flytrap leaf. The juices break down the insect's body, just as digestive juices in your small intestine break down foods. The leaf stays closed for 7 to 10 days. Then its hinge cells start losing water. As the cells become limp, the leaf begins to open. All that remains of the insect are tiny bits of its exoskeleton.

Reacting to the Environment

3

Metabolism: How Green Plants Function

All living things, including plants, need energy to stay alive. Whether they are trees like the spruces that grow in cold northern lands; cactus plants like the saguaros that live in hot, dry deserts; or African violets that live on windowsills, they need energy to grow and reproduce. They also need energy to take in gases from the air, water, and soil and to transport food and water throughout their bodies.

Plants get energy from food they manufacture. Making food, storing it, digesting it, and then breaking it down for energy are complex processes. Thousands of chemical reactions must take place. Together, these chemical reactions—plus all the other chemical activities that take place in a living organism—are called metabolism.

Metabolism is one process that distinguishes a living organism from a lifeless object. If it stops, the organism will die.

Opposite:
A garden comes alive with the blooms of hundreds of roses. By using light and water, green plants can produce their own food for energy.

Food Production and Storage

Each plant species has its own kind of leaves. Some leaves are long and skinny; others are very wide. Some have smooth edges; others have notched edges. But most leaves are thin and flat. Veins enter the leaves at the point where they attach to the plant's stem. These veins are part of the vascular system that carries materials from one plant part to another.

If you look through a microscope at the cross section of a leaf, you will see that the leaf is made up of millions of cells. The cells are arranged in several layers. On the top and the bottom is a thin layer of cells called the epidermis. The epidermis is covered with a waxy coat that protects the leaf and prevents water from leaving it. There are tiny holes in the epidermis, especially on the underside of the leaf. These holes are called stomates. Gases such as carbon dioxide, oxygen, and water vapor enter or leave the leaf through the stomates.

Two "guard cells" surround each stomate. The main job of the guard cells is to open and close the stomates. The guard cells close the stomates during

The Seediest Plants: Food Stealers

A few kinds of seed plants do not have chlorophyll, so they cannot make food. These plants, which are called parasites, steal their food from host plants. Taking a host's food can kill it.

Broomrapes are root parasites. They get all their food from the roots of other plants. A broomrape seed germinates, or begins to grow, only when it is near the roots of the right kind of host plant. When the seed germinates, the young broomrape immediately sends roots into a host's roots. The broomrape's roots grow until they reach the host's vascular system. Then food and water can pass from the host to the broomrape. No part of the broomrape appears above the ground until the plant is ready to flower. A fleshy shoot then emerges and grows upward. The flowering shoot may be yellow, red, brown, or even blue, but it is never green, because of its lack of chlorophyll.

Dodder

Dodders are stem parasites. They have long, thin stems that wind around the stem of a host plant, into which they grow root-like suckers. The suckers then join up with the host's vascular system and begin to remove food and water.

The Structure of a Typical Leaf

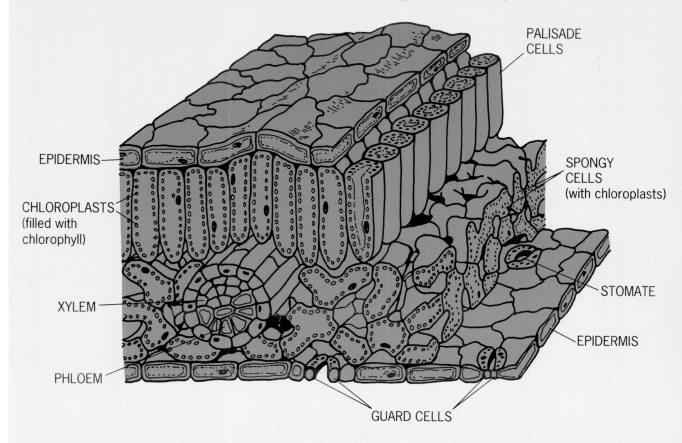

dry weather, thus preventing the leaf from losing too much water. At other times, the guard cells open the stomates so that gases can move in or out of the leaf.

Beneath the upper epidermis is a tightly packed layer of long cylinder-shaped cells called palisade cells. Each palisade cell contains many tiny green structures known as chloroplasts. Chloroplasts get their color from the substance called chlorophyll.

Between the palisade layer and lower epidermis is the spongy layer. Cells in this layer also contain chloroplasts, but there are lots of air spaces through which gases can easily move. Veins run through the spongy layer, too.

Within the veins are two kinds of tubes. Xylem tubes carry water and minerals from the roots to the leaves. Phloem tubes carry food from the leaf to the rest of the plant.

Metabolism: How Green Plants Function

A Sappy Story

Did you ever see buckets hanging from sugar maples in late winter and early spring and wonder why they were there? During this period, the tree's xylem tubes, whose role it is to carry water and minerals to the leaves, also carry sugars that have been stored in the tree during the winter. When this sweet sap starts running, people hang pails from the tree to collect it. Once it is collected, the sap is used to make maple syrup and other sweet products.

Photosynthesis Leaves—and in some plants, stems—produce food in the form of sugar for an entire plant. They are therefore the world's most important factories. Chlorophyll, a green substance found in plant leaves, allows the plants to make food. Plants, however, can produce food only in the presence of light, which is their source of energy. In addition, certain raw materials are needed, namely carbon dioxide and water. This food-manufacturing process is called photosynthesis. It means "putting together (synthesis) with light."

During photosynthesis, the light energy received by chlorophyll is trapped in the chloroplasts, which have gotten water from the veins and carbon dioxide from the air. The light energy splits the water in the chloroplasts into two parts: hydrogen and oxygen. First the oxygen is given off. Then the hydrogen quickly combines with carbon dioxide to form a simple sugar. In the process, the light energy is

The Process of Photosynthesis

To make its own food, a green plant needs three ingredients: water, carbon dioxide, and energy from light.

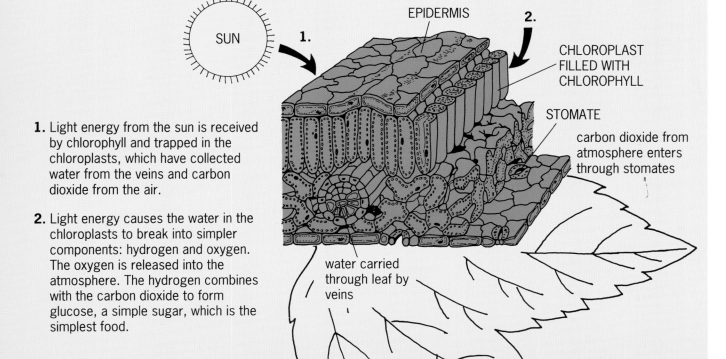

1. Light energy from the sun is received by chlorophyll and trapped in the chloroplasts, which have collected water from the veins and carbon dioxide from the air.

2. Light energy causes the water in the chloroplasts to break into simpler components: hydrogen and oxygen. The oxygen is released into the atmosphere. The hydrogen combines with the carbon dioxide to form glucose, a simple sugar, which is the simplest food.

EPIDERMIS

2.

SUN

1.

CHLOROPLAST FILLED WITH CHLOROPHYLL

STOMATE

carbon dioxide from atmosphere enters through stomates

water carried through leaf by veins

changed into chemical energy. This chemical energy holds the sugar molecules together.

Photosynthesis is the first step in food making. Plants can turn simple sugars into other substances, including complex sugars, starches, proteins, and fats. Once the food is made, the leaves send it to other parts of the plants through the vascular system.

Storing food A plant uses some of its food immediately, to build new cells and to provide energy. The rest of the food is kept for future use. It may be stored in any part of the plant. Usually it is stored in roots or stems. Carrot plants store food in their roots, while the baobab tree stores food in its huge trunk.

A plant also stores some food in its seeds. This food will be used by the new plants that grow from the seeds. They will get energy from the food until they can grow leaves and make their own food.

Plants take in more food than they can use at once and store reserves for future use. The baobab tree, for example, stores its extra food in its thick trunk.

Respiration

To stay alive, cells in all living things break down food to obtain energy. This process is called respiration. Respiration is the opposite of photosynthesis. While photosynthesis stores energy, respiration releases it. Photosynthesis makes sugar and gives off oxygen. Respiration uses oxygen to break apart sugar.

While photosynthesis takes place only in cells with chlorophyll, respiration takes place in every living cell. Moreover, photosynthesis takes place only in sunlight; respiration takes place day and night.

You take in the oxygen you need for respiration through your lungs when you breathe. A plant takes in its oxygen through the stomates in its leaves.

There are many chemical steps in respiration, but the result of this process is the same in animals and plants: sugar is broken apart, energy is released, and carbon dioxide and water are formed.

Metabolism: How Green Plants Function

4

Reproduction and Growth

The process by which new individuals of the same kind are produced is called reproduction. Reproduction is one of life's most important processes because it is necessary for the survival of any species. If members of a species do not reproduce, the species dies out, or becomes extinct.

One of the most productive of all plants is the dandelion. Each flower produces 200 or more seeds. It also has an excellent method of spreading these seeds. Each dandelion seed has a tiny parachute. When the wind—or a person—blows on a head filled with seeds, the seeds take off, drifting through the air. Eventually, the seeds fall to the ground, often far from the parent plants. Here, they grow into new plants. Because this small plant with its bright yellow flowers has literally traveled around the world, somebody once called it "the tramp with the golden crown."

Opposite:
Some of the most perfect partnerships in nature are between plants and insects. This pollen-covered flower beetle gets food from the daisy and, in return, it transfers pollen from one daisy to another—an essential part of the plant's reproductive process.

Mate Bait

Some species of orchids have a tricky way of attracting insects to help in pollination. The flower of the fly orchid actually looks and smells just like a female fly, wasp, or bee. Convinced that the fly orchid is a female of its species, a male insect lands on the flower and picks up pollen that sticks to its back and legs. When the insect flies off to another flower, the pollen is transferred, and pollination takes place.

All plants reproduce sexually by means of special structures: flowers, cones, or spore cases. Many plants can also reproduce asexually by structures such as runners that root in the soil.

Flowers

Flowers are the reproductive parts of flowering plants. They make the seeds that enable plants to produce more of their own kind.

Each kind of plant has its own special flowers. Some flowers are big and colorful; others are small and plain. Some flowers grow singly, and others grow in bunches. Some flowers open during the day; others open at night. Some are very fragrant, but many have no odor at all.

Even though they vary in many ways, all flowers have similar basic parts. The male parts of a flower are the stamens, which produce pollen. The female parts are the pistils, whose ovaries produce eggs. The flowers of some kinds of plants have both male and female parts—both stamens and pistils. In other kinds of plants, some of the flowers have only stamens and others have only pistils.

Pollination The first step in seed formation is the transfer of pollen from a stamen to a pistil. This is

Pollination Creation

Once upon a time the white flowers of brighamia were pollinated by an animal—probably an insect. No one knows for certain who the pollinator was because the species seems to have died out.

Without its pollinator, brighamia is also threatened with extinction. Only about 120 brighamia plants remain in the wild. They are found in Hawaii, on steep cliffs high above the Pacific Ocean. These few plants produce flowers, but because no animals carry the pollen from plant to plant, no seeds are produced.

Scientists are trying to save the brighamia. They climb the dangerous cliffs to pollinate the flowers. They use paintbrushes to carefully place pollen on the female parts of the flowers. This results in reproduction and the formation of seeds.

The Pollination Process

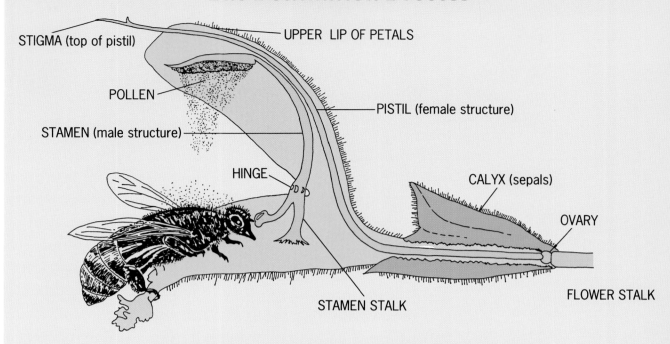

STIGMA (top of pistil)

UPPER LIP OF PETALS

POLLEN

PISTIL (female structure)

STAMEN (male structure)

HINGE

CALYX (sepals)

OVARY

STAMEN STALK

FLOWER STALK

The bee's head hits the stamen lever, which knocks pollen onto the bee's body. The bee will then travel to another flower and drop pollen on the pistil to pollinate other plants.

called pollination. Pollination may occur when pollen falls from a stamen onto a pistil of the same flower or onto a pistil of another flower on the same plant. Most plants, however, depend on animals or wind to carry pollen from one flower to another.

Dandelions, roses, and apples are among the many plants that are pollinated by animals. Insects such as bees, butterflies, and moths; birds such as hummingbirds; and bats are the most common pollinators. Flowers that depend on animals for pollination are brightly colored and often have a smell that animals like.

An animal visits a flower to feed on its pollen and to drink a sweet liquid called nectar. As the animal touches the flower, some of the pollen sticks to its body. When the animal leaves to visit another flower, it carries the pollen along with it. When it lands on a new flower, some of the pollen may rub off on the new flower's pistil.

DID YOU KNOW

Seeing Red

Many different kinds of animals pollinate plants. Aside from insects and birds, plants are pollinated by bats, mice, possums, and slugs. One way to tell which plants are pollinated by birds is to look at the color of their petals. Bright-red or pink flowers are the ones that attract birds the most, because birds have excellent color vision. Most insects cannot see the colors red or pink, so flowers with these colors are not often pollinated by insects.

Reproduction and Growth

His and Hers

To avoid self-pollination, the male and female parts of a flower—the stamens and the pistils—often mature at different times. When the stamens are ready to release their pollen, the stigma (tops of the pistils) are not ready to receive pollen. By the time the stigma are ripe and able to receive the pollen, the stamens have already shed all their pollen and have receded.

The largest fruit of any plant is produced by the jackfruit tree of Asia. One jackfruit can weigh as much as 65 pounds (29 kilograms).

The flowers of grasses, oaks, and birches use the wind for pollination. They do not need big, colorful, scented flowers. Their flowers are small, with long stamens that can easily be shaken by the wind. Their pollen is also very light, so it can be carried for long distances through the air.

Fertilization After pollen lands on top of a pistil, it forms a tube that grows down into the ovary. The ovary is the bottom part of the pistil, which contains the eggs. When a male cell, or sperm, from the pollen grain joins with an egg, the egg is fertilized.

The fertilized egg begins to grow, developing into an embryo. This is the first stage in the formation of a new plant. Together with all the surrounding food material, the embryo forms a seed. The ovary also grows and in time becomes a fruit containing one or more seeds.

Fruits and seeds Some plants, like pears and grapes, have large, juicy fruits. Snapdragons and maples have hard, dry fruits. The world's largest fruit is made by the jackfruit tree, which grows in southern

Asia. One jackfruit may weigh as much as 65 pounds (29 kilograms).

Seeds also vary in shape and size. Orchid seeds are no bigger than specks of dust. A pile of 1 million orchid seeds may weigh less than 1 ounce (28 grams)! Compare this with the nut produced by coco-de-mer trees, which grow on tropical islands. One coco-de-mer nut may weigh 40 pounds (18 kilograms).

Seeds from green plants vary greatly in size and weight. The nut of the coco-de-mer (*left*) can weigh up to 40 pounds (18 kilograms). An oak tree's nut, or seed (*above*)—commonly known as an acorn—will most often weigh only an ounce or two.

The number of fruits and seeds produced by a plant depends on the kind of plant, the amount of rain available, the temperature, and various other factors. In a year with good weather conditions, an oak tree produces about 50,000 acorns. Many of the acorns will be eaten by animals. Many more will fall in places where they cannot grow. Only a few will develop into new oak trees.

Germination When soil moisture, temperature, and other conditions are right, a seed begins to grow into a new plant. This process is called germination. The embryo root then breaks out of the coating that surrounds the seed and, using energy from food that is stored in the seed, grows longer. Soon, the first shoot pushes up through the surface of the ground. Leaves grow from the shoot, and the plant begins to make its own food.

Cones

Instead of flowers, pine trees and other conifers produce cones as their reproductive structures. A pine tree has two kinds of cones. Male cones are small, rather soft, and usually yellow or red. They form at the tips of branches in the spring. Female cones are large, woody, and brown. They consist of a series of shelf-like scales. The female reproductive organs containing eggs sit on top of the scales.

Pollen grains shed by the male cones are carried by wind to female cones. After sperm from the pollen grains fertilize the eggs, they develop into seeds. A conifer's seeds are exposed to the environment. They are not enclosed in a special structure such as a fruit.

When a seed is mature, it falls from the female cone to the ground and tries to germinate.

Pine trees and other conifers produce cones instead of flowers. The female cones, which are larger than the males, hold their eggs on the small shelves that make up each cone.

Spores

Ferns and mosses have complicated life cycles. They alternate between two kinds of reproduction. In one stage of their lives, they reproduce by spores. In the next stage, they reproduce by eggs and sperm.

Ferns If you look at the underside of a typical fern leaf, you are likely to see many dark brown dots. These are spore cases. Each case contains hundreds or even thousands of tiny spores. When the spores are ripe, the cases burst open, and the spores are released into the air or water.

When a spore lands in a damp, shady spot, it begins to grow. The plant that grows from the spore looks very different from a leafy fern. The new plant is heart-shaped and no bigger than your thumbnail. It has male and female structures that produce sperm and eggs. During wet weather, the sperm swim to the eggs, and fertilization takes place. Once this occurs, the fertilized eggs grow into leafy ferns.

Mosses You have probably seen moss plants on shady forest floors and in other damp places. These small plants grow very close together, covering the ground with soft, green carpets. Mosses produce sperm and eggs. When it rains and the plants become covered with water, the sperm swim from one moss plant to another, and fertilization takes place.

The fertilized moss egg stays on its parent plant. It grows into a new plant that is attached to the parent and gets its food from the parent. The new plant consists mainly of a brownish stalk and a spore case. When the spores are mature, the top of the spore case pops off. The spores are then carried away by wind. Spores that land on damp soil will soon develop into moss plants.

Spore cases line the back of a fern leaf. When the spores are ripe, the cases burst open. The spores are then carried by the wind to a damp, shady area, where they grow into a plant that produces both sperm and eggs.

Reproduction Without Seeds or Spores

Many plants reproduce asexually—without using seeds or spores. A strawberry plant, for example, sends out stems called runners that grow along the ground. Wherever a runner touches the soil, roots grow into the ground. Before long, new leaves form above the roots. The runner connecting the parent plant to the baby plant dies away. Soon the baby plant is big enough to send out its own runners.

Producing a new plant from part of an old plant is called vegetative reproduction. Some of the food plants you eat are grown in this way. Look closely at a potato. It has many little "eyes." These are buds. Farmers cut a potato into pieces so that each piece has a bud. They plant each piece, which grows into a new plant. Energy needed for this growth comes from food stored in the potato.

The banana plant's stem is underground. What appears to be the plant's trunk—more than 30 feet (9 meters) high—is actually formed by the bases of overlapping leaves. Like the potato, a banana-plant stem can be cut into pieces so that each piece has a bud. Roots and leaves will then grow from the buds.

Potatoes are among the many vegetables that reproduce by way of vegetative reproduction. This means that new plants are produced from parts of an old plant. The "eyes" of each potato sprout buds that can be planted to grow new potatoes.

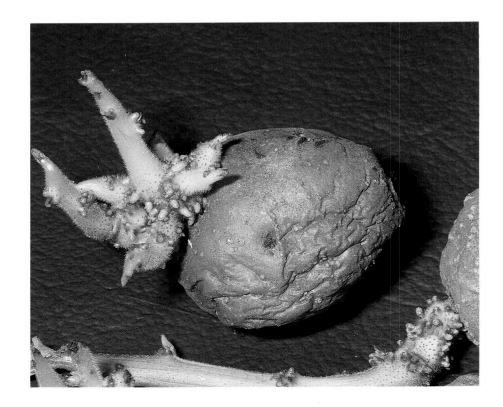

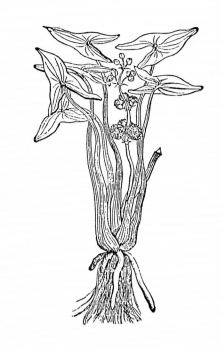

Cutups

Coleus is a popular houseplant with pretty red and green leaves. Here's how you can have a whole windowsill filled with coleus—and have enough plants left over to give as presents!

Remove a stem from a coleus plant. Choose a stem that has at least three or four leaves. Put the stem in a glass of water. Place the glass in a light place but not in direct sunlight.

Within a few days you should begin to see tiny roots growing from the stem. In about two weeks, when there are many roots, put your cutting in a flowerpot filled with soil. Place the flowerpot in a sunny area, and keep the soil damp. Soon you will have a nice big plant with many colorful leaves.

Other plants can also be started from a stem that has its leaves attached. Begonias and geraniums are popular examples. There are even some plants, such as African violets, gloxinias, and jade plants, that can be started from a single leaf.

A number of plants can also be started from roots. Cut off the top inch or two of a fresh carrot. Place the piece, cut end down, in a shallow dish. Add enough water to cover about half the carrot top. Soon the top will sprout leaves. It's then ready to be planted in some soil.

Plant Growth

Fifty years ago, a young boy carved his initials on the branch of a tree near his home. Today the tree is much taller. The branch is much longer, but it is the same height above the ground as it was 50 years ago. The initials can still be seen—exactly where the boy carved them. Why didn't the initials move as the branches extended outward?

Growth does not take place evenly throughout a plant. There is no lengthwise growth in old parts. Lengthwise growth occurs at the tips of roots and stems. Cells in the tips divide over and over again, producing new cells. This makes the roots and stems longer, while the older parts remain where they were.

The branch on which the boy carved his initials may be in the same place today as it was 50 years ago, but it is much wider. The tree trunk is also wider. In tree trunks and branches there is a layer called the cambium, which lies between the xylem and the phloem. Cambium is a growth tissue. As it grows, it makes new xylem and phloem—xylem on the inside, and phloem on the outside. Old xylem becomes wood. This causes the tree to grow in diameter—that is, it grows wider.

Old phloem becomes bark. Bark is a tree's skin. It protects the tree from attacks by animals and disease-producing organisms. It also protects the tree from drying out. Bark isn't as wide as the woody inner

Trees grow in layers made up of cambium, xylem, and phloem. By "reading" a tree's layers, a person can tell how old a tree is, what has happened to it during its lifetime, and what weather conditions were like for each year the tree was alive. Here, a 1,710-year-old sequoia trunk is labeled to show how thick it was during various ages in the past.

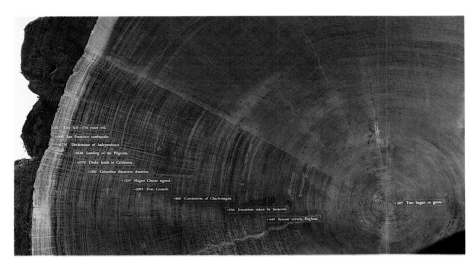

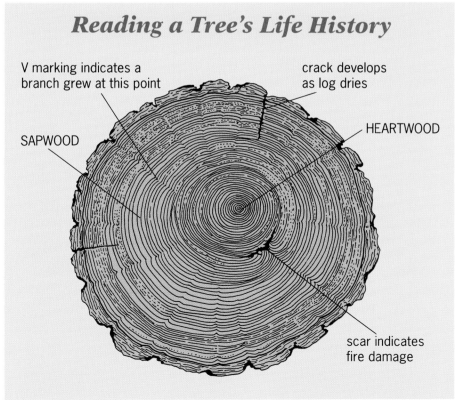

Reading a Tree's Life History

V marking indicates a branch grew at this point

crack develops as log dries

SAPWOOD

HEARTWOOD

scar indicates fire damage

Cross Section of an Elm-Tree Stem

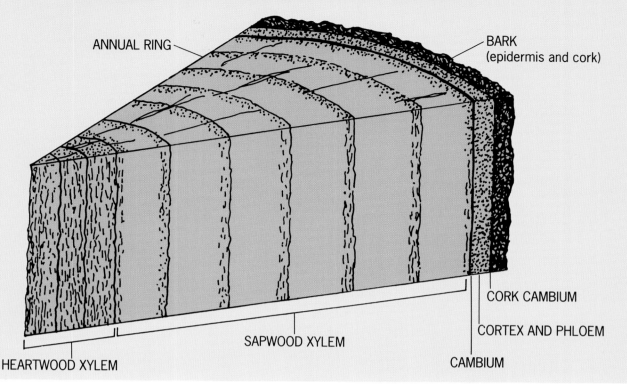

ANNUAL RING

BARK (epidermis and cork)

CORK CAMBIUM

CORTEX AND PHLOEM

CAMBIUM

SAPWOOD XYLEM

HEARTWOOD XYLEM

parts, because the dead outer layers of bark wear off or fall off—just like the dead outer cells of your skin. Each year, the cambium layer in a tree's trunk and branches grows a new layer of wood just underneath the bark. This new wood looks like a ring. The light part of the ring is made in the spring, and the dark part is made in the summer.

By counting the rings in a tree stump, you can tell the tree's age. You can also learn something about the weather from these rings. In a year with plenty of rain, growth is fast, and the ring is wider than usual. In dry years, growth is slow, and the ring is narrow.

Light, temperature, and soil conditions also affect tree growth. A young pine tree, for example, that is growing in the shade of older pines will grow more slowly than it would if the other trees weren't there. Cut down the older pines, and the young pine will receive much more sunlight. This will allow the tree to grow at a faster rate, and the rings that are formed will be wider.

DID YOU KNOW

Growing in Circles

Scientists once counted the rings of a giant sequoia that had been destroyed by fire in the mid-1900s. They determined that the tree was 2,048 years old when it died. It was a young tree when Julius Caesar was born in 95 B.C., but by the time Christopher Columbus arrived in the Americas in 1492—almost 1,600 years later—its trunk was 9 feet (3 meters) wide! It continued to grow, adding another ring each year, until the fire killed it.

Fitting into the Web of Life

Coconut palms cover islands in the South Pacific. Edelweiss, with its white, woolly flowers, decorates some rocky mountains in Switzerland. Cacao trees, from which chocolate is made, grow in Brazil's rain forests. Cattails thrive in swamps and moist ditches in North America.

Each kind of plant has adaptations that help it live in a certain kind of environment. Coconut palms have adaptations that help them live on tropical islands. These palms would die if they were planted on a Swiss mountain.

What determines the types of plants that live in a particular place? Light, rainfall, winds, temperature, and soil conditions are critical factors. The activities of other plants and animals—including people—are also of major importance.

Opposite:
A Guadalupe rain forest is thick with vegetation. Rain forests are some of the most productive areas on Earth—environments where thousands of species of living things thrive together.

The saguaro, found in the desert of the American Southwest, is one of the world's biggest and longest-lived cactuses. A 250-year-old saguaro can be 50 feet (15 meters) tall, can weigh 6 tons (5 metric tons), and can store enough water in its stem to keep it alive for about three years.

Adaptations for Different Climates

Deserts are very dry. They receive little rain, but when rain does fall, carpets of tiny plants suddenly appear. One of these plants is the bladderpod mustard. Rain causes the mustard's seeds to germinate. The young plants grow quickly, producing flowers, which, in turn, produce a new crop of seeds. This entire life cycle—from seed to flower to seeds—may be completed in only 10 days, or the seeds may lie in the ground for years, waiting for the next rain.

Unlike most plants, cactuses, which live mainly in dry places, make food and store water in their thick stems rather than in leaves. The thin spines on their stems help to prevent water loss. A cactus also has a system of many long roots. The roots grow very close to the surface, spreading widely in all directions. They can soak up water quickly, even after a very light rainfall. The water that is stored in the stem is used during dry periods. For example, the giant saguaro cactus can store enough water in its stem to last the plant about three years.

At the opposite extreme are living conditions in tropical rain forests. Some of these forests receive

Getting Antsy

Need protection? How about getting some ants? That's what Mexico's bullhorn acacia does.

The bullhorn acacia has two long, hollow spines at the base of each leaf. A certain kind of ant lives in these spines. The ants feed on sweet juices that are produced by the acacia and, in exchange for free food and a place to live, the ants protect the acacia. They sting insects and other animals that try to eat the acacia. They also bite off the stem tips of other plants that grow too close to their hosts.

Bullhorn acacias that have ants to protect them are healthy and grow well, but if the ants die, so do the trees.

hundreds of inches of rain every year. Plants have large, wide leaves with many stomates so they can easily give off excess water.

Trees in a tropical rain forest are evergreen. That is, they are always green and keep their leaves all year long. Tropical evergreens also grow all year round. Other trees, such as maples and oaks, which are common to cold climates like the Canadian forests, are deciduous. These trees lose all their leaves in autumn. Their branches are bare until the following spring, when they grow a new set of leaves. Trees cannot grow when temperatures fall below freezing. Their roots cannot take in water when the ground is frozen, so maple and oak trees rest until spring, when days are once again warm. They shed their leaves to protect against losing water. During their winter rest, the trees do not carry out photosynthesis—instead, they depend on their stored food to stay alive.

How Plants Defend Themselves

When a zebra spots a hungry lion, it uses its strong legs to run away. Plants, however, cannot escape enemies by running. They have other adaptations to protect themselves.

Have you ever brushed your hand or leg against a stinging nettle? If so, you'll never forget the experience! The stinging nettle is a rather ordinary-looking plant that grows among grasses and weeds in fields and along roadways. It is covered with many tiny hollow hairs. At the base of each hair is a container filled with poison. When you—or an animal—brush against the nettle's hairs, the tips break off. The hairs enter the skin, and poison flows into your body. The sting caused by these tiny "needles" lasts for hours.

Many plants have sharp spines on their stems or leaves. This prevents animals from eating the plants.

Plants, Petals, and Poisons

Although many plants are valuable sources of food and medicine, many others can be quite dangerous and even deadly.

Castor-oil, which comes from the beans of the castor-oil plant, has been drunk for generations as a way to rid the body of toxins. But these beans also contain ricin, which is one of the strongest poisons known. The amount of ricin in just one bean is enough to kill a human being.

Other plants are also known to cause harmful effects in humans if eaten. If the sap of the dumb cane is eaten, its poison causes enormous swelling in the mouth. The victim's mouth often swells so much that he or she is unable to speak, which explains the plant's name. Belladonna, or deadly nightshade, is another plant whose leaves are highly poisonous if eaten. Even the pit of a delicious peach contains some arsenic, which is a potent poison to humans.

Deadly nightshade

Castor-oil plant

Dumb cane

Holly trees, yuccas, and roses are examples of plants with this kind of special defensive adaptation.

Plants have to defend themselves against other plants, too, preventing them from "stealing" their water and other resources. The leaves of the brittlewood shrub secrete a poison. Rains wash the poison off the plant's leaves and onto the ground. The poison makes the soil near the shrub so deadly that other plants cannot grow there.

Fire is another enemy of plants. Many plants are killed by fire, but their seeds are able to survive. One reason that sequoias can live for thousands of years is that they can defend themselves against fire with their thick bark. Some old sequoias have bark that is 2 feet (0.6 meter) thick!

Stinging nettles are covered with many tiny, hollow hairs that break off and release poison into the skin of an attacker.

Stick with the Butterwort

The butterwort—which grows in swampy, marshy areas—has layers of flat, harmless-looking leaves. But each leaf is actually covered with a sticky glue that traps insects and keeps them stuck to the surface until they die. Once an insect is dead, the butterwort's leaves slowly curl inward, and the animal is digested.

Fly trapped by butterwort

Leaves of Three, Let It Be!

Poison ivy

When Europeans first arrived in North America, Native Americans told them not to touch a small creeping plant with shiny three-part leaves because the plants would cause a nasty, painful itch.

This plant—poison ivy—is still a problem. Poison ivy contains an oil called urushiol, very little of which is needed to produce a skin rash. The amount of urushiol that fits on the head of a pin is enough to cause rashes in 500 people!

Poison oak is a relative of poison ivy. It also has three-part leaves filled with urushiol. When you walk through fields and forests, in parks, or along roadsides, watch out for poison ivy and poison oak. A brush with them could leave you itching to get home!

A Hair-Raising Experience

Some plants, like the sundew, grow in areas where the soil does not contain enough minerals. To obtain these minerals, the plants eat insects. When an insect visits the sundew plant, the sticky hairs on its leaves trap the insect. Fluid from the plant then covers the insect, preventing it from breathing. The insect dies, and the sundew produces juices that help it digest the insect.

The Human Connection to Plants

Look around you. How many plants are part of your daily life? A good place to start counting is in the refrigerator!

As you have learned, people depend on green plants for food. When you eat apples, cereals, lettuce, and walnuts, you are eating parts of plants. Tea, coffee, vegetable oils, spices, sugar, and chocolate also come from plants. When you eat meat, such as a hamburger, you are indirectly getting food from plants; the hamburger is made from the flesh of cattle that ate grass and hay.

As you have also learned, people rely on plants for the oxygen in the atmosphere. The oxygen that is released into the air during photosynthesis is the most essential element in sustaining human life. But this relationship is not simply a one-way street. In fact, plants benefit from humans and other animals, just as humans benefit from plants. As part of respiration, oxygen is breathed in, but carbon dioxide is breathed out as a waste gas. Carbon dioxide is the gas—together with water—that is necessary for photosynthesis. In this way, the waste product of one organism becomes a life-sustaining element for another. That's why the interdependence between plants and animals is perhaps the most beautiful of all relationships in nature.

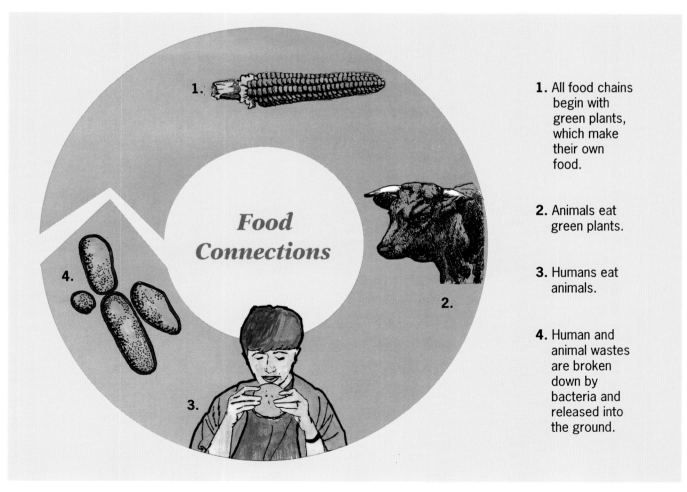

Food Connections

1. All food chains begin with green plants, which make their own food.

2. Animals eat green plants.

3. Humans eat animals.

4. Human and animal wastes are broken down by bacteria and released into the ground.

The dried leaves of the foxglove plant provide digitalin, an effective heart medicine.

People have many additional uses for green plants. Trees supply lumber for buildings and furniture, paper for books and newspapers, and wood for stoves and fireplaces. Cotton plants provide fibers used for clothing, and rubber trees give us rubber. Lavender, roses, and other sweet-smelling flowers provide oils used in perfumes.

Plants Save Lives

Some of our most valuable medicines also come from plants. The bark of the cinchona tree is the source of quinine, a medicine used to treat malaria. The dried leaves of foxglove provide digitalin, an important heart medicine. The rosy periwinkle gives us medicines used to treat certain kinds of cancer.

People have studied the chemical properties of only a tiny percentage of plants. They are continuing to find new medicines in plants. It is possible that many more plants than we are aware of produce chemicals that could cure human illness. This is one of the reasons it is important for people to take good care of the environment and the plants within it.

Besides serving many life-sustaining functions, green plants are valued for their beauty. People place

A Rosy Outlook

Rose hips

When the ovules in a rose plant become fertilized and turn into seeds, the receptacle that holds them begins to swell and turn red. When the receptacle is ripe, it is known as a rose hip. Rose hips have proven to be helpful to humans in maintaining good health. Because they contain up to 100 times more vitamin C than any food, they have been used to make vitamins and other products that work to prevent colds and other illnesses. Many people believe that rose-hip tea also helps to keep the bladder and kidneys healthy.

Natural fibers produced by plants—such as cotton—are a valuable source for clothing and other cloth or canvas goods.

potted plants and cut flowers in homes, schools, and offices to dress up their surroundings. Homeowners and businesses plant trees, shrubs, and flowers to decorate their grounds.

Trees are also planted in yards and in parks to provide shade. Some people even use trees as a source of enjoyment—kids hang tires and swings from trees, build houses in them, and climb them.

When people harm or destroy natural habitats, many plants are left to struggle for survival. Some species become threatened with extinction. When a species becomes extinct, people can no longer enjoy its beauty or benefit from its chemicals, fibers, or stored food.

It may seem funny, but some people actually talk to their plants. They talk to plants growing on their windowsills and in their gardens. Do you talk to plants? What do you say to them? If you think of all the wonderful things that plants do for people, you might want to say "thank you."

DID YOU KNOW

When Plants Are Animals

Plants may not be animals, but people have found a way to carve many shrubs into bears, elephants, dogs, and lots of other creatures. This art form is called topiary. Topiary is actually garden sculpture. Anyone with a little creativity and talent and a pair of pruning shears can carve all sorts of shapes out of greenery—not just animals.

Classification Chart of Green Plants

Kingdom: Plantae

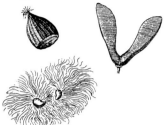

Scientists have identified about 400,000 species of green plants. These species are classified in groups according to their structure. All the species in a group share certain characteristics that make them different from species in other groups. Scientists do not always agree on how plants should be grouped. As a result, there are different classification systems. Here is one common classification system for the main kinds of green plants.

Major Group	Common Members	Distinctive Features
Bryophyta "moss plants"	true mosses, liverworts, hornworts	small plants with no vascular tissue; reproduce by spores; usually live in moist places
Pterophyta "wing plants"	ferns	vascular plants with feathery leaves called fronds; reproduce by spores that form on undersides of leaves
Coniferophyta "cone-bearing plants"	conifers (pines, firs, spruces, yews, cedars, sequoias, and others)	vascular trees and shrubs with needle-like or scale-like leaves; reproduce by seeds that usually form on cones
Anthophyta "flower plants"	flowering plants	vascular plants; seeds are enclosed in a fruit that forms from the ovary of the flower

Flowering Plants

The division Anthophyta is the largest group of plants, with about 250,000 known species. Scientists have classified these species into families. There are more than 300 families of flowering plants. The following are 14 of the most familiar families.

Major Family	*Common Members*
Aceraceae maple family	box elder, hornbeam, maple, sycamore
Arecaceae palm family	coconut palm, date palm
Cactaceae cactus family	cactus, night-blooming cereus, opuntia
Compositae composite family	aster, chrysanthemum, dahlia, daisy, dandelion, goldenrod, lettuce, sunflower, thistle, zinnia
Cruciferae cabbage family	alyssum, broccoli, cabbage, cauliflower, radish, stock, turnip, watercress
Gramineae grass family	bamboo, barley, bluegrass, corn, millet, oats, pampas grass, rice, rye, sugarcane, wheat
Labiatae mint family	bergamot, lavender, peppermint, salvia
Leguminosae legume family	acacia, alfalfa, bean, clover, lupine, mimosa, pea, peanut, soybean, sweet pea, wisteria
Liliaceae lily family	aloe, amaryllis, asparagus, garlic, hosta, hyacinth, lily, onion, Solomon's seal, tulip, violet
Orchidaceae orchid family	orchids
Rosaceae rose family	apple, blackberry, cherry, mountain ash, pear, plum, raspberry, rose, spiraea, strawberry
Rubiaceae madder family	cinchona, coffee, gardenia, madder, woodruff
Solanaceae potato family	capsicum (chili), eggplant, henbane, mandrake, petunia, potato, thorn apple, tobacco, tomato
Umbelliferae carrot family	anise, caraway, carrot, celery, fennel, parsley, parsnip

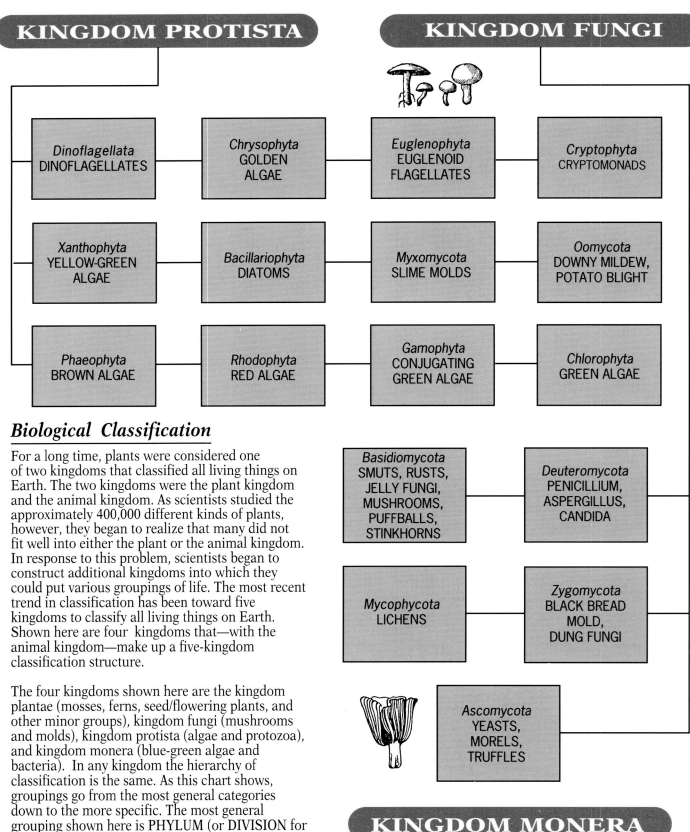

KINGDOM PROTISTA

Dinoflagellata DINOFLAGELLATES	*Chrysophyta* GOLDEN ALGAE	*Euglenophyta* EUGLENOID FLAGELLATES	*Cryptophyta* CRYPTOMONADS
Xanthophyta YELLOW-GREEN ALGAE	*Bacillariophyta* DIATOMS	*Myxomycota* SLIME MOLDS	*Oomycota* DOWNY MILDEW, POTATO BLIGHT
Phaeophyta BROWN ALGAE	*Rhodophyta* RED ALGAE	*Gamophyta* CONJUGATING GREEN ALGAE	*Chlorophyta* GREEN ALGAE

KINGDOM FUNGI

Basidiomycota SMUTS, RUSTS, JELLY FUNGI, MUSHROOMS, PUFFBALLS, STINKHORNS	*Deuteromycota* PENICILLIUM, ASPERGILLUS, CANDIDA
Mycophycota LICHENS	*Zygomycota* BLACK BREAD MOLD, DUNG FUNGI
Ascomycota YEASTS, MORELS, TRUFFLES	

KINGDOM MONERA

Schizophyta BACTERIA, BLUE-GREEN ALGAE

Biological Classification

For a long time, plants were considered one of two kingdoms that classified all living things on Earth. The two kingdoms were the plant kingdom and the animal kingdom. As scientists studied the approximately 400,000 different kinds of plants, however, they began to realize that many did not fit well into either the plant or the animal kingdom. In response to this problem, scientists began to construct additional kingdoms into which they could put various groupings of life. The most recent trend in classification has been toward five kingdoms to classify all living things on Earth. Shown here are four kingdoms that—with the animal kingdom—make up a five-kingdom classification structure.

The four kingdoms shown here are the kingdom plantae (mosses, ferns, seed/flowering plants, and other minor groups), kingdom fungi (mushrooms and molds), kingdom protista (algae and protozoa), and kingdom monera (blue-green algae and bacteria). In any kingdom the hierarchy of classification is the same. As this chart shows, groupings go from the most general categories down to the more specific. The most general grouping shown here is PHYLUM (or DIVISION for plants). The most specific grouping listed is ORDER. To use the chart, you may want to find a familiar organism in a CLASS or ORDER box and then trace its classification upward until you reach its PHYLUM or DIVISION.

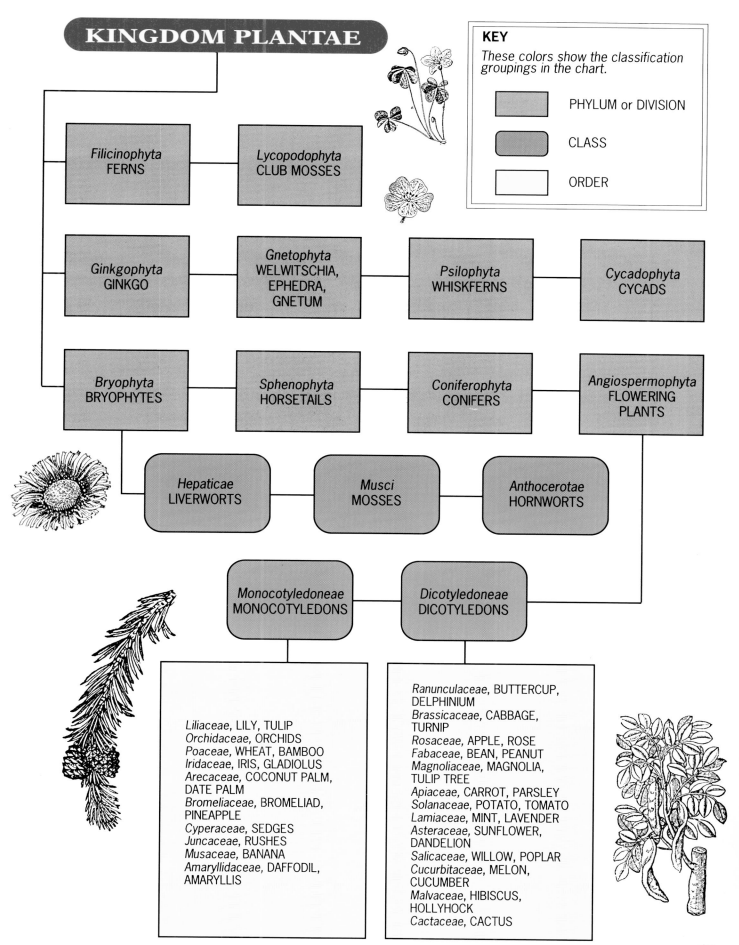

KINGDOM PLANTAE

KEY

These colors show the classification groupings in the chart.

PHYLUM or DIVISION

CLASS

ORDER

Filicinophyta FERNS

Lycopodophyta CLUB MOSSES

Ginkgophyta GINKGO

Gnetophyta WELWITSCHIA, EPHEDRA, GNETUM

Psilophyta WHISKFERNS

Cycadophyta CYCADS

Bryophyta BRYOPHYTES

Sphenophyta HORSETAILS

Coniferophyta CONIFERS

Angiospermophyta FLOWERING PLANTS

Hepaticae LIVERWORTS

Musci MOSSES

Anthocerotae HORNWORTS

Monocotyledoneae MONOCOTYLEDONS

Dicotyledoneae DICOTYLEDONS

Liliaceae, LILY, TULIP
Orchidaceae, ORCHIDS
Poaceae, WHEAT, BAMBOO
Iridaceae, IRIS, GLADIOLUS
Arecaceae, COCONUT PALM, DATE PALM
Bromeliaceae, BROMELIAD, PINEAPPLE
Cyperaceae, SEDGES
Juncaceae, RUSHES
Musaceae, BANANA
Amaryllidaceae, DAFFODIL, AMARYLLIS

Ranunculaceae, BUTTERCUP, DELPHINIUM
Brassicaceae, CABBAGE, TURNIP
Rosaceae, APPLE, ROSE
Fabaceae, BEAN, PEANUT
Magnoliaceae, MAGNOLIA, TULIP TREE
Apiaceae, CARROT, PARSLEY
Solanaceae, POTATO, TOMATO
Lamiaceae, MINT, LAVENDER
Asteraceae, SUNFLOWER, DANDELION
Salicaceae, WILLOW, POPLAR
Cucurbitaceae, MELON, CUCUMBER
Malvaceae, HIBISCUS, HOLLYHOCK
Cactaceae, CACTUS

Glossary

adaptation A structure or behavior that helps an organism survive in its environment.

algae Simple microscopic organisms, most of which live in water.

auxin The chemical within a plant that causes the plant to bend.

cambium The layer of a tree's trunk and branches located between the xylem and the phloem.

cell The microscopic unit that is the building block of all living things.

cellulose The material of which plant walls are composed.

chlorophyll A green substance found in plant cells that is needed for photosynthesis.

chloroplasts Tiny green structures within plant cells, where photosynthesis takes place.

conifer A cone-bearing tree.

deciduous plant A plant that loses its leaves in winter.

embryo A young developing organism.

epidermis An outer layer of cells.

evergreen A plant that is green year-round and that does not lose all its leaves in winter.

evolve To change over a long period of time.

extinct No longer in existence.

fertilization The union of sperm and egg, which leads to the development of a new organism.

flagella Tail-like structures of certain one-celled organisms.

fossil The preserved record of an organism that lived long ago.

germination The growth of a seed into a new plant.

gravitropism Bending in response to gravity; also called geotropism.

gravity A force that pulls objects toward Earth.

host plant A plant from which another plant steals nutrients.

metabolism The chemical processes in cells that are essential to life.

molecule The smallest particle of a substance that retains all the properties of a substance.

ovary A female structure that produces eggs.

palisade cells Cylinder-shaped cells beneath a leaf's upper epidermis.

parasite An organism that lives in or on another organism.

phloem The part of a plant's vascular system that carries food through it.

photosynthesis The process by which green plants make food.

phototropism Bending in response to light.

pistil The female part of a flower.

pollination The process by which pollen is transferred from the male part of a flower to the female part of a flower.

reproduction The process by which organisms create new members of their species.

respiration The breaking down of food to obtain energy.

species A group of organisms that share more traits with one another than with other organisms and that can reproduce with one another.

sperm The male reproductive cell that fertilizes a female egg.

spores The reproductive structures of ferns and mosses.

stamen The male part of a flower.

stigma The top of a flower's pistil that receives pollen grains.

stimulus A change in the environment that can be detected by an organism.

stomates Tiny holes in a leaf's epidermis through which gases enter and leave.

tap root A large main root of some plants.

tendrils Special stems or leaves that curl around a support.

topiary The art of training, cutting, and trimming trees or shrubs into ornamental shapes.

tropism A movement in response to a stimulus.

turgor movement A movement that depends on changes in internal water pressure.

urushiol The oil in poison ivy and poison oak.

vascular plant A plant with a system of tubes that carry water and food throughout the plant.

vegetative reproduction Producing a new plant from part of an existing plant.

xylem The part of a plant's vascular system that carries water and minerals through it.

For Further Reading

Behme, Robert L. *Incredible Plants: Oddities, Curiosities & Eccentricities*. New York: Sterling, 1992.

Burnie, David. *Plant* (Eyewitness Books). New York: Alfred A. Knopf, 1989.

Burnie, David. *Tree*. New York: Knopf Books for Young Readers, 1988.

Collinson, Alan. *Grasslands*. New York: Macmillan Children's Group, 1992.

Dowden, Anne O. *Plants That Harm & Heal*. New York: HarperCollins Children's Books, 1994.

Facklam, Howard, and Facklam, Margery. *Plants: Extinction or Survival?* Hillside, NJ: Enslow, 1990.

Greenaway, Theresa. *Ferns*. Madison, NJ: Raintree Steck-Vaughn, 1992.

Greenaway, Theresa. *Fir Trees*. Madison, NJ: Raintree Steck-Vaughn, 1990.

Greenaway, Theresa. *Mosses & Liverworts*. Madison, NJ: Raintree Steck-Vaughn, 1992.

Greenaway, Theresa. *Woodland Trees*. Madison, NJ: Raintree Steck-Vaughn, 1990.

Harlow, Rosie, and Morgan, Gareth. *Trees & Leaves*. New York: Franklin Watts, 1991.

Johnson, Sylvia. *Mosses*. Minneapolis, MN: Lerner, 1983.

Leggett, Jeremy. *Dying Forests*. North Bellmore, NJ: Marshall Cavendish, 1991.

Madgwick, Wendy. *Cacti & Other Succulents*. Madison, NJ: Raintree Steck-Vaughn, 1992.

Madgwick, Wendy. *Flowering Plants*. Madison, NJ: Raintree Steck-Vaughn, 1990.

Nations, James D. *Tropical Rainforests: Endangered Environments*. New York: Franklin Watts, 1988.

Nielsen, Nancy J. *Carnivorous Plants*. New York: Franklin Watts, 1992.

Pope, Joyce. *Plant Partnerships*. New York: Facts On File, 1991.

Ricciuti, Edward R. *Plants in Danger*. New York: HarperCollins Children's Books, 1979.

Tesar, Jenny. *Endangered Habitats*. New York: Facts On File, 1991.

Tesar, Jenny. *Shrinking Forests*. New York: Facts On File, 1991.

Warburton, Lois. *Rainforests*. San Diego, CA: Lucent, 1991.

Index

Photo Credits